soddet

First published 2020

Text copyright © 2020 Greg Tustain
Illustrations copyright © 2020 Harry Wyld
SODDET is a trade mark of Greg Tustain

All rights reserved.

The right of Greg Tustain and Harry Wyld to be identified
as the author and illustrator of this work has been
asserted by them in accordance with the Copyright,
Designs and Patents Act 1988. No part of this publication
may be copied, reproduced, stored in or introduced into
a retrieval system or transmitted in any form, or by any
means, without the prior permission of Greg Tustain and
Harry Wyld, nor be otherwise circulated in any form of
binding or cover other than that in which it is published
and without a similar condition being imposed on the
subsequent purchaser.

ISBN: 979-8-5658913-0-0

INTRODUCTION 3

CURRENT UNFAIRS
FAKE OFF 6
IF NOT 8
STATUE TORY 10
BULLSHIT BINGO 13
WHICH 1? 14
LIFE'S A BEACH 17
RISK REWARD 18

EVERY DAY ISSUES
COFF UP 22
OUTSIDE LANE 25
HUG. UGH. 26
GETTING PERSONNEL 29
JAM DOUGHNUT 30
GOOD GRIEF 33
ROUND 'EM UP 34

FIENDS OF THE EARTH
DOG FLOWER 38
THE JETSAM SET 41
REVERSE PSYCHO 42
BLUE FIELDS 45
A COUNTRY PILE 46
TMI 49
FLY BYE 50

ALL THE RAGE
NECROTISING FASHIONITIS 54
TIME GENTLEMEN 57
LAMB DRESSING 58
DIAMONDS ARE A FEVER 61
GOODBYE! 62
ON BALANCE 65
CROSS KEYS 66

THE STATE OF THE ARTS
YES, TODAY 70
SELFIE ABUSE 73
MY PRIVATE VIEW 74
SCREENED OFF 77
QUESTIONABLE TIME 78
BRAVO OSCAR 81

BAD SPORT
EFF ONE 84
TALENT POOL 87
ALTIUS-ISH 88
MAN U 91
GREEN EYES 92
THE WORM-CAST 95
WHAT'S THE POINT? 97

LAST WORDS
TIME WASTING 100

INTRODUCTION

This book should be a leaflet. When I wrote
My debut rhyme, I meant to stop right there.
I thought that only one thing got my goat
Sufficiently for me to give it air.
Apparently I'm not quite that laid back.
It turns out I'm becoming more unfair,
And I'm ashamed to say I can attack
Inconsequential failings anywhere.
You'll sometimes see my tongue is sticking out,
While other times it's in the cheek, concealed.
You may agree or want to rage and shout
At me. Alas, my spleen remains unsealed,
So you will find (OK, I'm no King Lear)
Iambic pent-up anger venting here.

CURRENT UNFAIRS

FAKE OFF

We know from school that rulers should be straight,
But now we've had to kick that into touch.
We're finding out a vote or two too late
The biggest of them all don't care too much
For honest truth. They blur and turn and twist
Their lines until they can't be understood
By millimetre people. What we missed -
An honest, fair debate - has gone for good.
We know they'll lie away at us from here
On in, with news that makes us lie awake
At night. And we are filled with real fear -
The only real thing when facts are fake.
For in these thiefdoms, what they take away
Is everything we valued yesterday.

IF NOT

Could someone please unpack the maths? I've tried
To make the numbers add up, but they don't.
Some natural justice has to be applied.
It doesn't help that law enforcement won't
Gain all the access needed to arrest
The heroes of these money-shuffling deals.
They played it hard and failed the basic test;
They need to know how destitution feels.
But that will never happen. In their game
Of triumph and disaster, gain and loss,
They treat those twin imposters just the same -
They carry on and never give a toss.
Such smugness when they've got the whole thing wrong!
Bet half the morons end up with a gong.

STATUE TORY

Right, shoulders back and spread your legs, Jack. Cheese!
You're in 'The Power Set'. But don't believe
That stupid stance looks strong. We're bound to tease
You, trying to look steadfast, sure, as we've
Seen stronger paper bags. Don't bother us
With image - it's an idiotic pose
That you must strike, just like rhinoceros,
Immovable, legs splayed, and no one knows
Quite why. Extinction can't be far away,
And fear cannot be made to disappear
Behind the rictus grin you now display.
You know that there's another new career
More fitting for a legs-spread statuette?
With five peers you could form 'Jack's Croquet Set'.

BULLSHIT BINGO 💩

I try so hard to turn the other cheek
And shut my ears to phrases sprayed about
Like cluster bombs of clever. This technique
Of saying something - anything - no doubt
Impresses idle listeners who pray
For just one thing: that they won't need to speak.
But what do all these keynote speakers say
While paddling all the way up bullshit creek?
They think outside the box, they raise the bar
And going forward try to win-win bizz
Then circle back to fill the cookie jar
With twaddle talk. So it is what it is
And every TV interview confirms
The phrase that's Number One, in terms of terms.

WHICH 1?

A niggling issue exercising folk
Around the world is how the money's shared.
They quote the figures, saying it's a joke,
And how the yawning gulf should be repaired.
Yes, 99% of all the wealth
Is in the hands of 1%. Indeed.
And we are short of funds to pay for health,
Policing, housing and the rest. Agreed.
We're short because another 1%
Cost 99 times more to keep at bay;
I mean the baddies. Good folk strive, but bent
Men live beyond our means - it is the way.
Lambast the 1% who laugh at law -
Their rackets make them rich and make us poor.

LIFE'S A BEACH

Our bouncing babies cannot hope to hide
Their wide-eyed wonder when they see the sea.
They splash and paddle, podgy, mystified
How such a great big bath exists, while we
Lie back upon the cold wet sand. We know
This time is short and soon we'll have to tell
The truth we'd love to hide: that H_2O
Supports all life and bouncing bombs. Farewell
To hazy hopes, once shiny but now fast
Dissolving on the huge horizon, where
The future lies in wait to steal the past
From children. We can hear their first despair
As daytime heat descends to evening chill.
"Why does the walk home have to be uphill?"

RISK REWARD

Icelandic banks. Remember them? They broke.
And RBS? It disappeared as well.
The savers saw their wealth go up in smoke
As rich career execs fell into hell.
Er, no. The lines above were never set.
The Government and Central Bank roared in
To underwrite the gamblers' massive debt.
But it's a game that only bankers win.
We make decisions based on what we know
About the world, and then the powers that be
Move goalposts; risk and profit rules all go.
When they were irresponsible, whoopee!
They were 'too big to fail' - too big to bleed -
And what were we? Too tiny to succeed?

EVERY DAY ISSUES

COFF UP

I'd like a pound for every time I've seen
Commuters with that strangely branded juice
Of over-priced arabica - the bean
That thinks it's worth it - playing fast and loose
With hard-earned cash. I cannot bear to pay
A hundred times above the instant rate
Before I've even hit the working day.
I can't start three or four pounds down. No, wait,
That's six - those muffins look too good to miss -
And if I'm feeling really daft, I'll try
A shot of caramel. We think, as this
Is coffee, it is healthier to buy
Than English breakfast. Ah, but which is worse?
The coffee, for your waistline and your purse.

OUTSIDE LANE

Well look at you, you clever thing. You know
That no one overtakes you; after all
The limit is your rapid seven-o.
Those people stretched behind you have some gall
To think they can go faster, but they can't
Because there is a law. They can't pretend
It's not there, and we know full well you aren't
About to break it now. So that's the end
Of it. You stubborn little jerk. Just look
Left mate, and see the empty lanes where you're
Supposed to be. Or might the coppers book
You for allowing us to speed? I saw
You glancing in your mirror. Let me pass
Before I ram my bonnet up your arse.

HUG UGH.

I hear new music every day and try
To teach my ears to like it. But I'm told
We know the soundtrack of our story by
The time we're thirty, and as we grow old
New tunes all sound like squeaky blackboard chalk.
The same is true for etiquette, you know.
We men shake hands as soon as we can talk
And think both skills are good for life. But throw
Away such misconceptions, sad old git,
And throw your arms around all those you meet -
A metro fad that's not affection, it
Is affectation. Catch me in the street
And I will make it plain I'm not a fan.
You really shouldn't try to hug me, man.

GETTING PERSONNEL

A supermarket boss - don't know his name -
Was on the radio. I'm sure I heard
Him say his colleagues all deserved acclaim
For working through the virus. Oh that word.
Not virus. No no. Colleague. Must we bear
Such PC HR tosh? The NHS
Has porters, nurses and consultants. They're
All 'staff', all heroes who could not care less
For titles, while the supermarket team
Of top consultants plumped for 'colleague' since
It smacks of equals. But what can redeem
The 'Colleague (ugh) Announcement'? (Hear me wince?)
You'll see me as pernickety, I think,
But every little helps me to the brink.

JAM DOUGHNUT

Oh good, a rush hour single file that crawls
Along at thirteen mph. And now
I'm watching as my speedo gently falls
To middle single figures. Holy cow!
There goes the bedtime story and the song;
The dinner will be warm but not as good
As when it was created. Is this long
And winding queue because of work that should
Have taken place at night? Or has a horse
Escaped its field? Or has there been a prang?
A festival or sports event? Of course
I should have known it. I would like to hang
The one-eyed two-wheeled free-from-scruple dicks
Who think they own the road at ten to six.

GOOD GRIEF

I planted fruit and veg this year to live
The Good Life; I'd make gingham-labelled wine,
Jam, chutney, cider and the rest to give
As tasty little treats for friends of mine.
I hear it's what the country life's about.
But nature raises two green fingers each
And every afternoon I venture out
To tackle bits of garden. I beseech
You, what am I supposed to do out here
Now harvest time has come? I need a list,
But thirst things first, I think I need a beer…
Mistake. I now see piles of fruit I missed
And mellow fruitfulness can really niff,
Attracting king-size wasps which scare me stiff.

ROUND 'EM UP

A candid but informal game we play
When drinking in a group is 'Who Will Buy?'
I hope I'm not describing you here: "They
Think others do not notice when they try
To wriggle out of paying." How we laugh
As culprits slope off loo-ward, or protest
That last time round they only had a half,

Or pat their pockets, looking down. The best
Of them are masters of their chosen art
(At least the suckers like to think they are)
As we're left helpless, watching them not part
With folding any time they're at the bar.
For heaven's sake, stop cheating, buy the beers,
Then go and sit down over there pal. Cheers.

FIENDS OF THE EARTH

DOG FLOWER

I caught a teasing flash of shiny black
While marching past the brambles and the sloes
That filled the hedgerow. Quickly I turned back,
The twitcher in me twitching in the throes
Of uncontainable excitement. I
Have ticked off all the native birds, but there
Within the bush was something that my eye
Could not believe. It wasn't, sadly, rare
At all, but still it's hard to classify
Such dumb stupidity: a bag of shit
Tied tidily and then suspended by
The seldom-spotted Common Little Tit.
We ring the legs of birds, but what the heck -
With tits like this, we need to wring the neck.

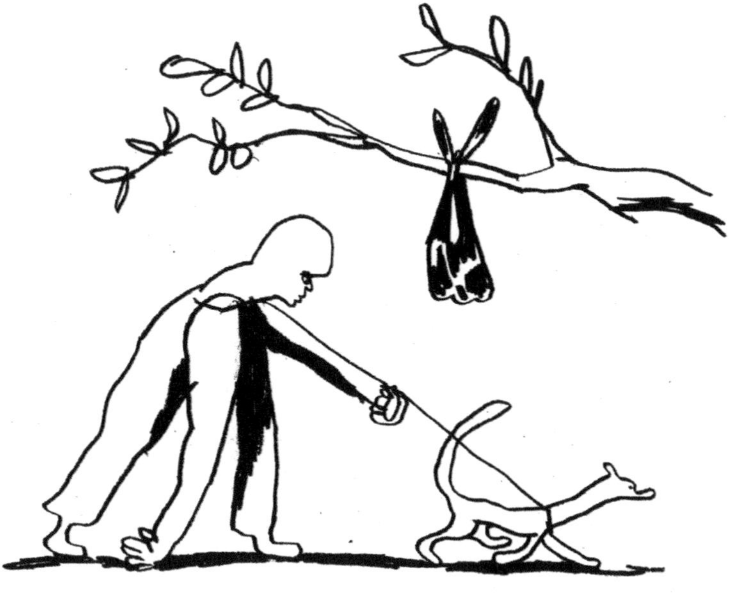

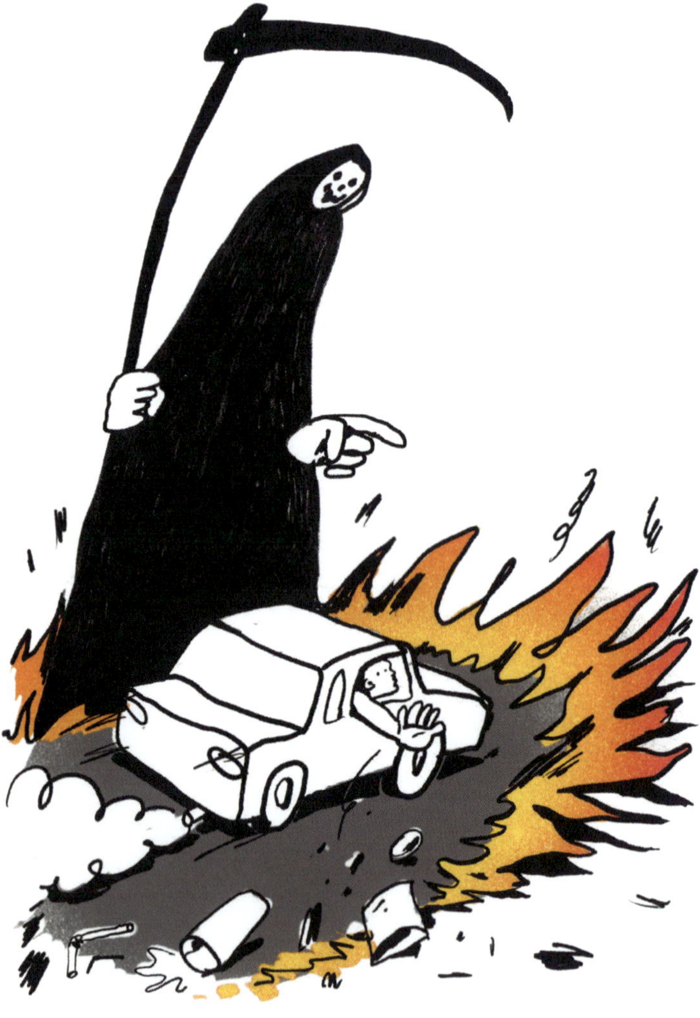

THE JETSAM SET.

For modern living, not much can compare
With burgers on a motorway. A neat,
Efficient, drive-through-one-shop-stop from where
You race, your laptop food now primed to eat
Within a minute. Progress has become
A multi-tasking life spent in the feast
Lane, seasoned and unleaded, with the hum
Of other fast-track diners driving east
But quickly heading south. Now what to do?
You know a tidy car's a tidy mind
So post your rubbish through your window - you
Proceed while your detritus stays behind.
It will not rot, but I am bound to tell
You that you will. When you arrive in hell.

REVERSE PSYCHO

There goes that sound again - the tiresome beep
You hear whenever someone backs a truck.
I blame those Health and Safety folk who keep
On making laws and couldn't give a beep
About intrusive sounds and how they grate.
But this reversing thing's a different class;
From miles away the piercing pings create
A pain that works its way right up your beep.
I used to love the walk past Greengate Farm
Identifying birds among the flock
Of Romneys, but the tractor's shrill alarm
Now tortures twitchers. What a load of beep.
There was a risk with happy living once
But beeps have beeped it up, the beeping beeps.

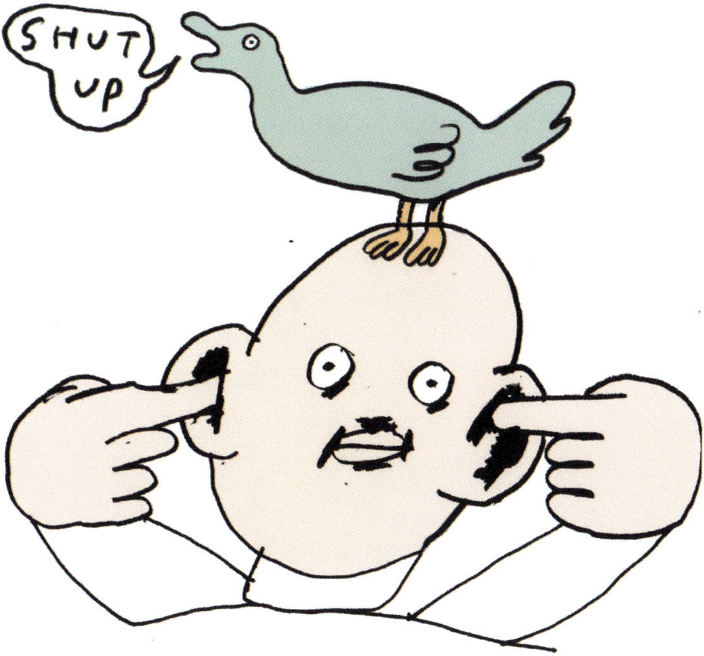
SHUT UP

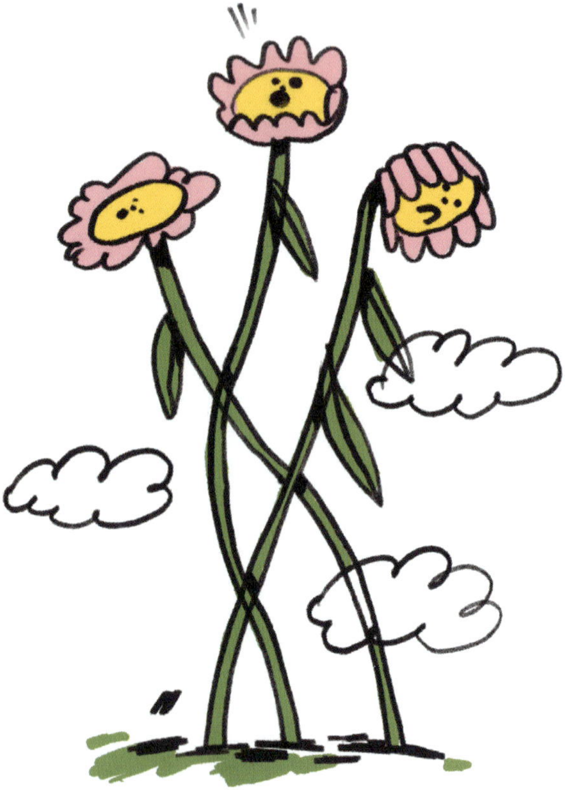

BLUE FIELDS

We know spring fields are green. We learn in youth
A timeless fact that others learned before.
But now they teach just one eternal truth:
We die. Those fields will soon be green no more.
For others who retread our footsteps here
The crops will be a scientific blue -
All sterilised and disinfected, clear
Of withering disease. These pastures new
Once looked like greener grass beyond the fence
But still we haven't learned that lesson well
Enough. How come we do not have the sense
To call a halt as we plough into hell?
Around blue fields as once-green elders die
The orange elder spurns the reason why.

A COUNTRY PILE

A stroll in fenland paradise, I thought,
Until I saw a mountain rising. Eh?
That's odd - no plate tectonics could have wrought
Such wicked devastation in a day.
A spur of sofa, ridge of bath, arête
Of mattress and a north face wardrobe door
Assembled there deliberately, yet
This was no Gormley, Hirst or Henry Moore.
Our sculptor had misread the artist's call
To break down fences. He had used a van
Backed up with fully-comp insurance (wall
Of darkness, ease of getaway, big man)
To cast his artwork. How much pleasure it
Would give me to exterminate the shit.

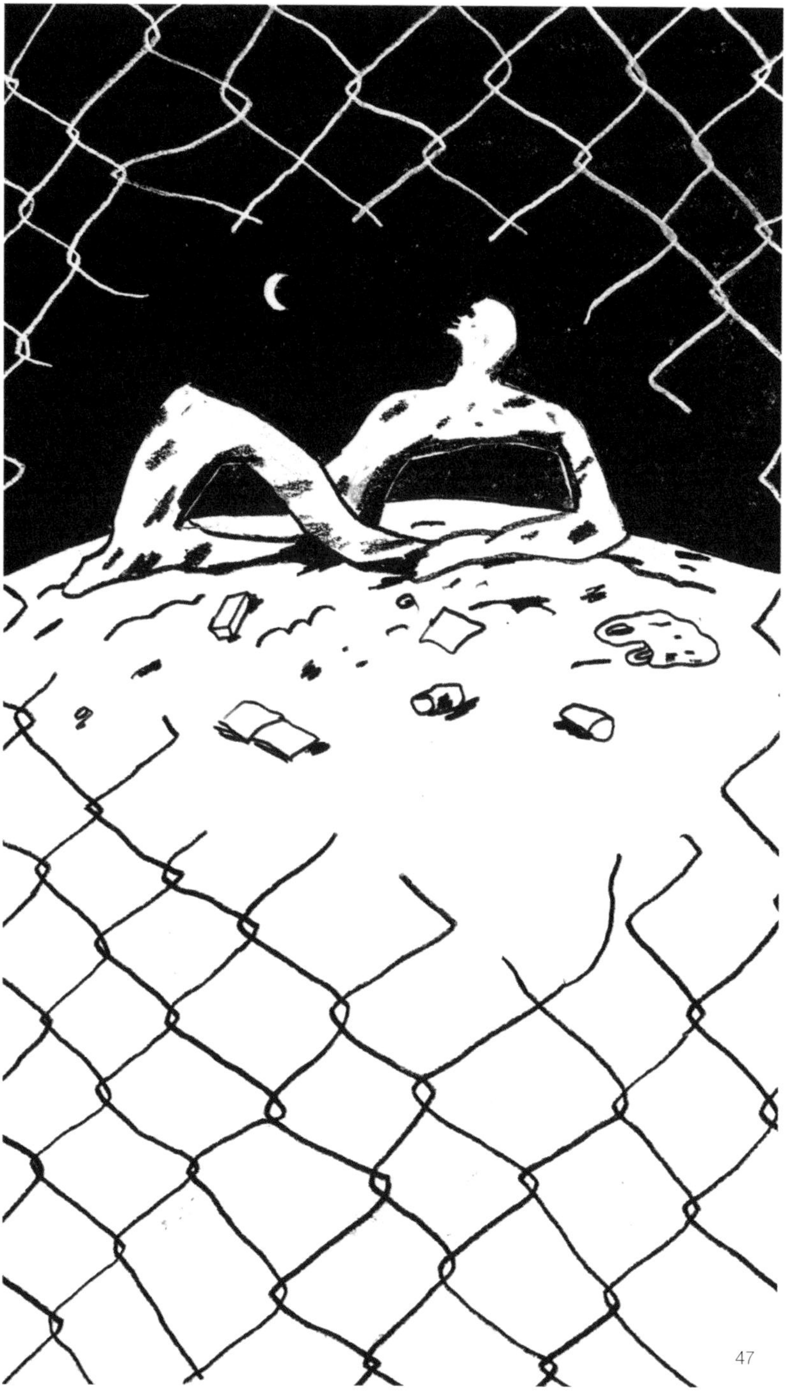

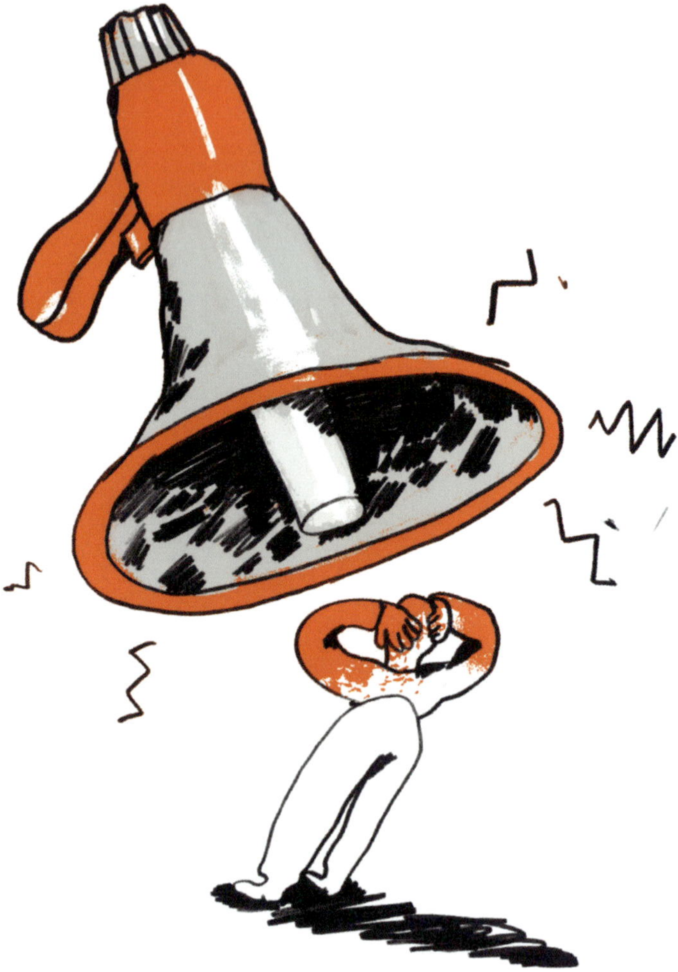

TMI

The shouting signs - too many for the wall -
Go head-to-head with eardrum-numbing waves
Of idiot announcements. What's it all
About? We listen/look as each word saves
Us from apparent danger everywhere,
But we cannot hear/see what chaos is
Out there because these statements clog the air,
These slogans cloud the glass, their messages
Dismissed as info fog, misheard/misread
By mystified ears/eyes, beyond the bounds
Of valuable suggestion, written/said
As Public Informationless Sights/Sounds.
It's crucial work, the agencies all say,
But they're P-I-S-S-ing it away.

FLY BYE

When measured pound for pound, of all the beasts
Awarded points for pissing people off
The housefly must come first. See how it feasts
On all your body matter; watch it scoff
Its way through your... perhaps I'll leave that there.
My major grievance with the buzz-filled squit
Is how it thrives in numbers anywhere
You want to spend some pleasure time. And it
Apparently derives as much as you
By screwing yours up. Irritating pest.
My children say - because I've killed a few -
That I'll come back as one when laid to rest.
I hope they're right. I think I would enjoy
Life if He said "Now go forth and annoy."

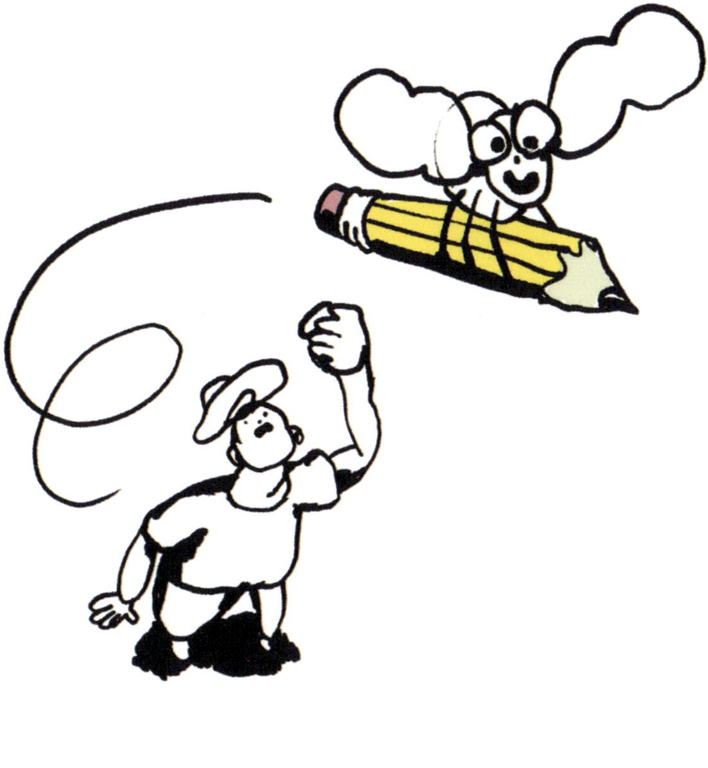

ALL THE RAGE

NECROTISING FASHIONITIS

I don't suppose it comes as a surprise
To hear I'm short on fashion sense - I buy
What's practical. Of course I realise
I'm just a little out of touch, but why
Should I keep up when cool is cold next day?
I'd feel a fool to follow. Then again,
It's fun for fashionistas - they can play
At it and change their look completely when
They choose. You can't play with tattoos. They're in
Right now and, just like any other fad,
They'll soon be out again. But printed skin
Cannot be thrown in drawers. It's not so bad
To see the shoulder-captured little birds,
But bramble-strangled limbs? I have no words.

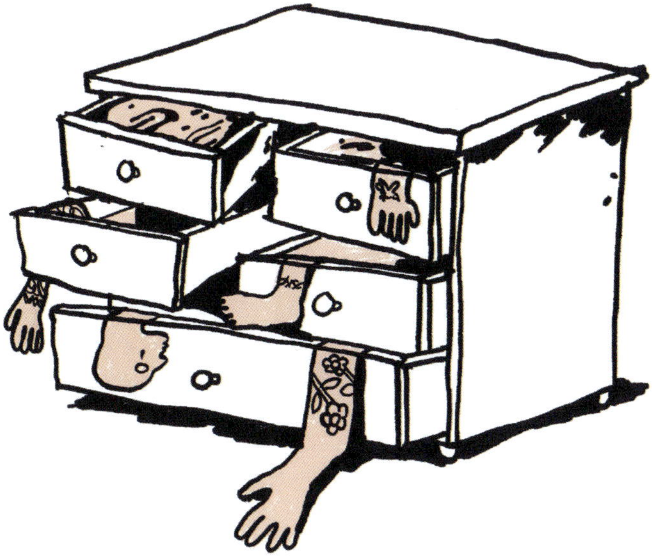

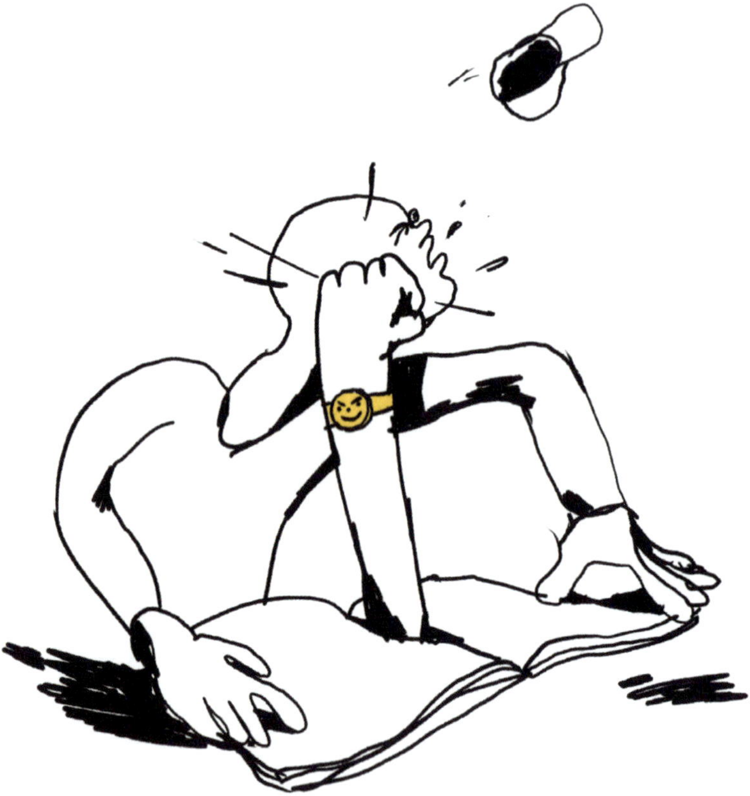

TIME, GENTLEMEN

Too often when I turn the final page
Of any supplement or magazine
I have to clench my teeth to stop the rage
I should be flying into having seen
Another one of those pathetik ads
Where future perfect model and his watch
With young male heir beside him shows us dads
How he has lifted manhood up a notch
Or two but I have yet to see the wife
Who I suspect has long since done a bunk
In search of someone who can share her life
Far from our 2-D onanistic hunk.
I need to take a breath. You get the gist -
His heart's desire is on and off his wrist.

LAMB DRESSING.

A strange sight troubled me today. I saw
A blonde young beauty. From behind, she looked
As perfect as can be. I was in awe.
I tried to look away but I was hooked.
Her chauffeur held the door and touched his hat
As she stepped out and slowly turned around,
While I felt frozen stupid where I sat.
My Venus had four legs - an Afghan hound.
I mention this because I've seen a wave
Of long blonde hair on every other head;
That rarity most men and women crave
Is now - if not abundant yet - widespread.
I don't know why, but it is strange to see
A blonde can be a lass of 83.

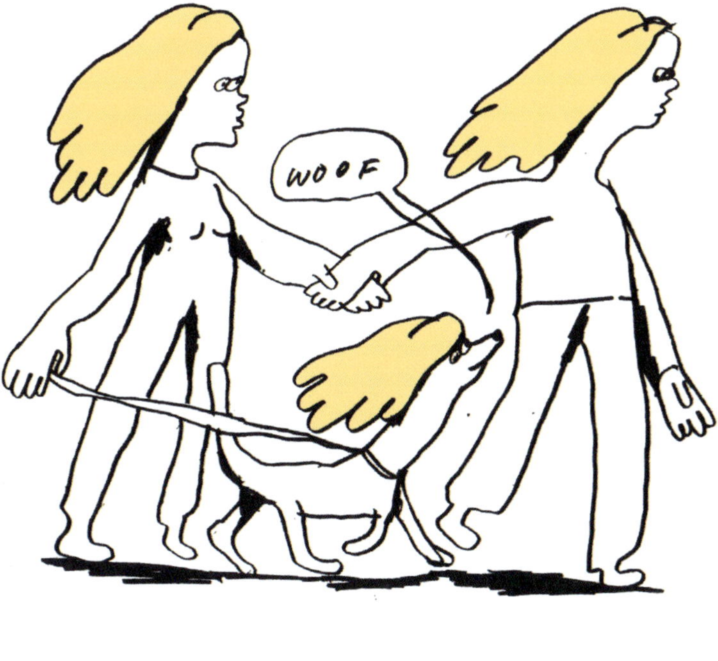
WOOF

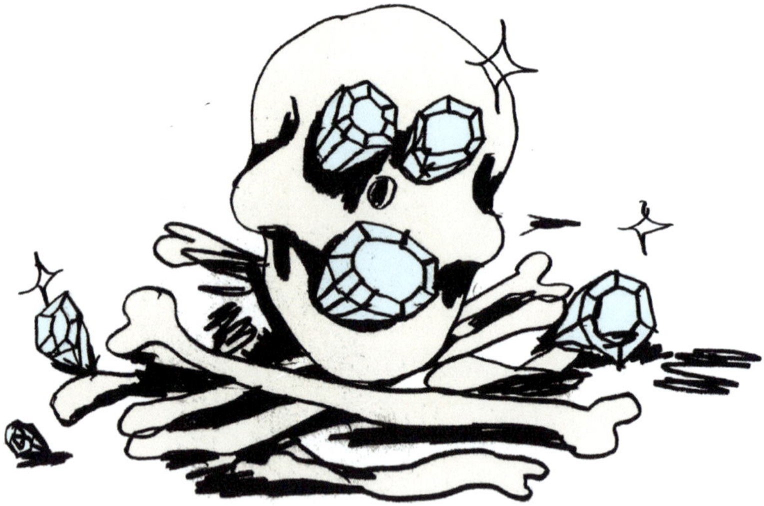

DI◆MONDS ARE A FEVER

A huge dynastic fortune has been made
In precious gems - its name will always mean
the Best. And looking closely at their trade,
A greater triumph there has never been.
I mean of marketing. The enterprise
Itself, we hear, is not quite laissez-faire,
(Allegedly they cap their own supplies),
But now we can make rocks from carbon, they're
Contending 'natural' value is a fact.
The lover-buyer's passion sizzles, but
I'm no romantic; stones can be pre-packed
With Colour, Carat, Clarity and Cut -
The famous Cs. How splendidly they shone.
But now we add another C-word. Con.

~~GOODBYE!~~

"Hello! I'm in an LBD today.
I say 'today', but you will know I mean
The next few minutes. Just until they say
They have the shot, and then I'll change. You've seen
Our fifteen-bedroom house? I'm very proud
Of all the alterations - in and out.
I have an eye, you see, and watch the crowd
Keep up. Another shot? Another pout?
Of course. No point in staying still, unless
I'm talking of my constant friend and rock.
We've recently renewed our vows, and yes
I wore the same dress, which was quite a shock
For everyone who came. They know of course
I'm his for life." Hello! Sounds like divorce.

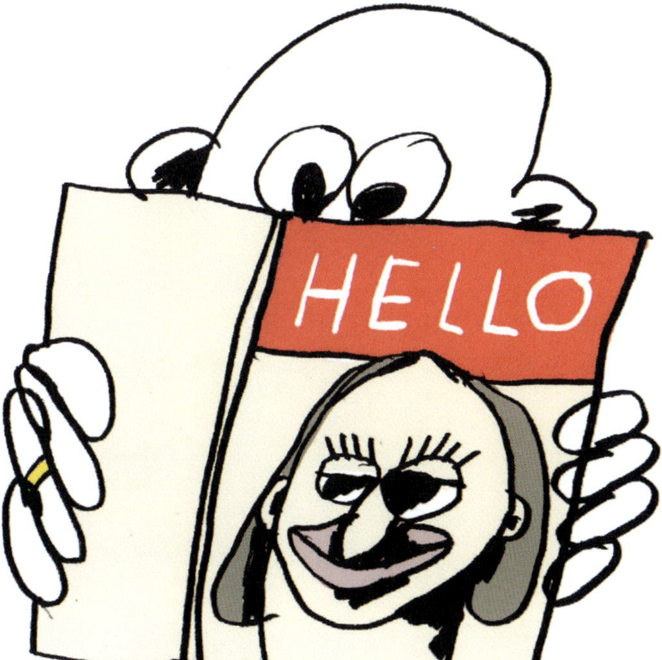
HELLO

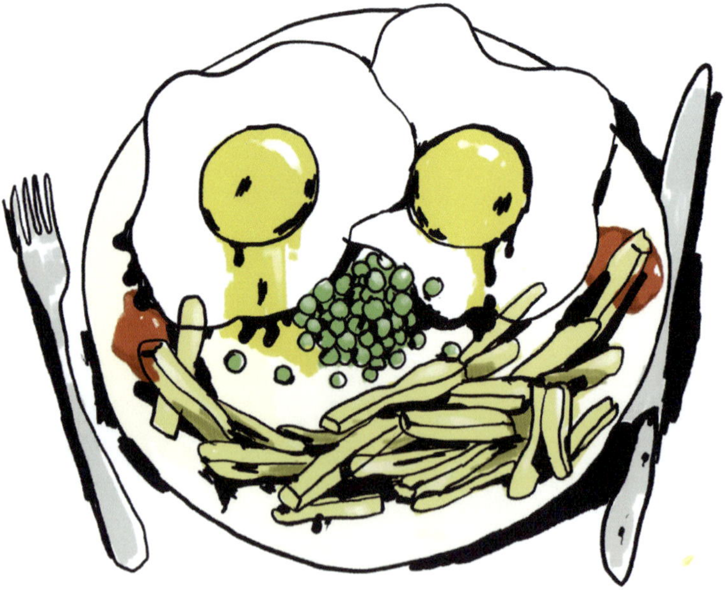

ON BALANCE

It's true (says some new study out today)
That we're less prone to accidents if we
Have just a little drink. Hip hip hooray!
But alcohol's a public enemy -
We all know that. And Christiaan Barnard said
That smoking four or five a day is fine
If giving up might see your nerve-ends shred
Themselves. Now what? *No sugar! Don't combine
Your fats and carbohydrates! You should try
The Atkins! Cambridge! Vegan!* But they ought
To show more balance, so on balance I
Dismiss each vested interest report
As partial nonsense. Read my greasy lips:
I'm partial to a curate's egg and chips.

CROSS KEYS

My favourite pastime - going down the pub -
Is not the pleasure that it used to be
When it was drinking only. Now that grub
Has had to take the leading role, I see
My local is a bistro, with no space
For all the finer things in life, like darts
And pints and conversation. It's a place
That used to hum with chat and fags; now farts
(Be they man-made or veggie-cooked) are king.
The menu choice is endless - patience must
Be too - as microwave alarm bells ring
Each time they turn a foreign dish to dust.
I want a beer. And if I need to eat,
A roll and stew would make the finest treat.

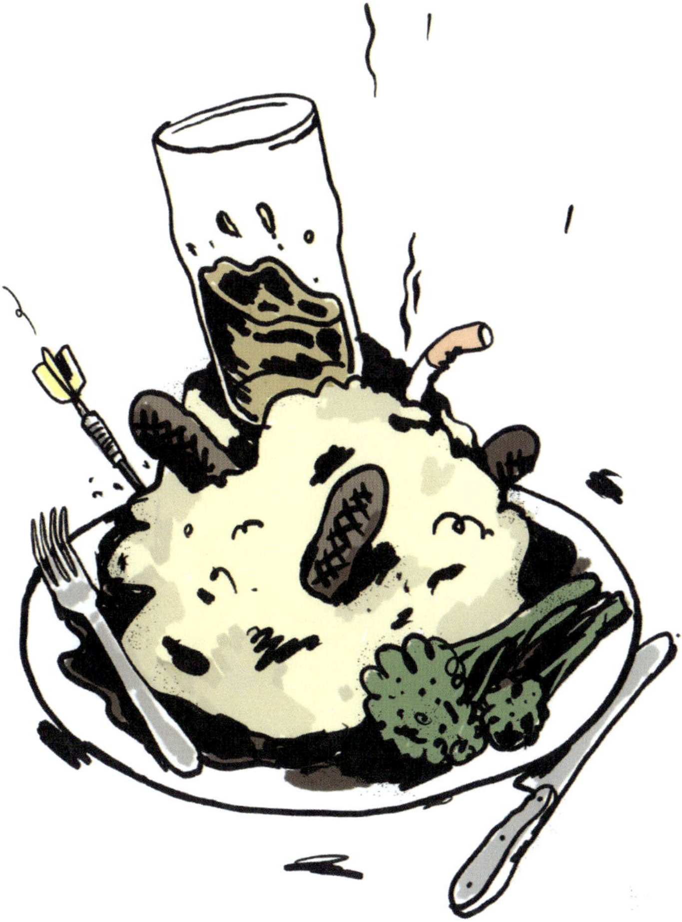

THE STATE OF
THE ARTS

YES, TODAY

"Now with us in the studio today
We have Professor Smith, who leads the field.
All controversial stuff, it's fair to say?"
"It started…" "Yes, I think your work revealed
That we become frustrated when we face
An interviewer champing at the bit
To have his voice heard; he won't leave a space
And interrupts incessantly." *"Permit
Me please to clari…"* "If I may, we've learned
Of course, you have a vested interest here -
You chair the free speech pressure group, and earned
A tidy little sum from them last year."
"I don't get pai…" "Oh really? No big bunce?"
Keep quiet, you anchor. Listen up for once.

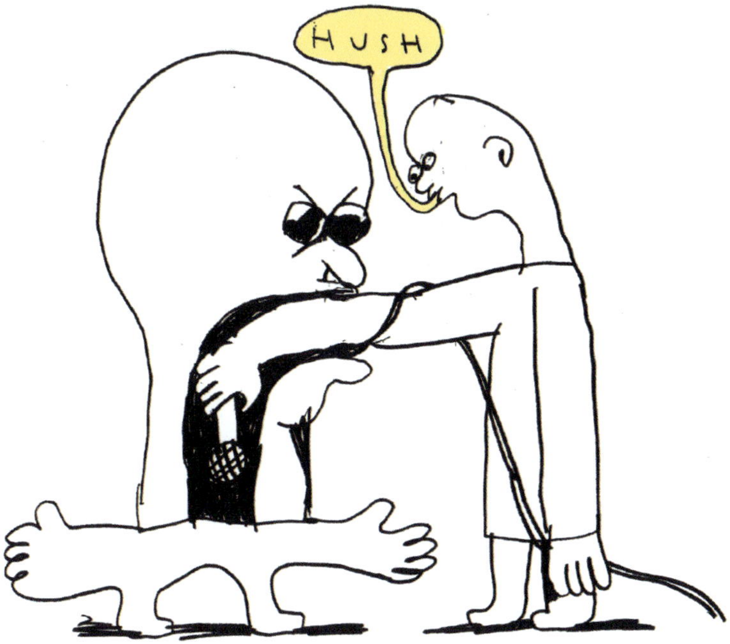
HUSH

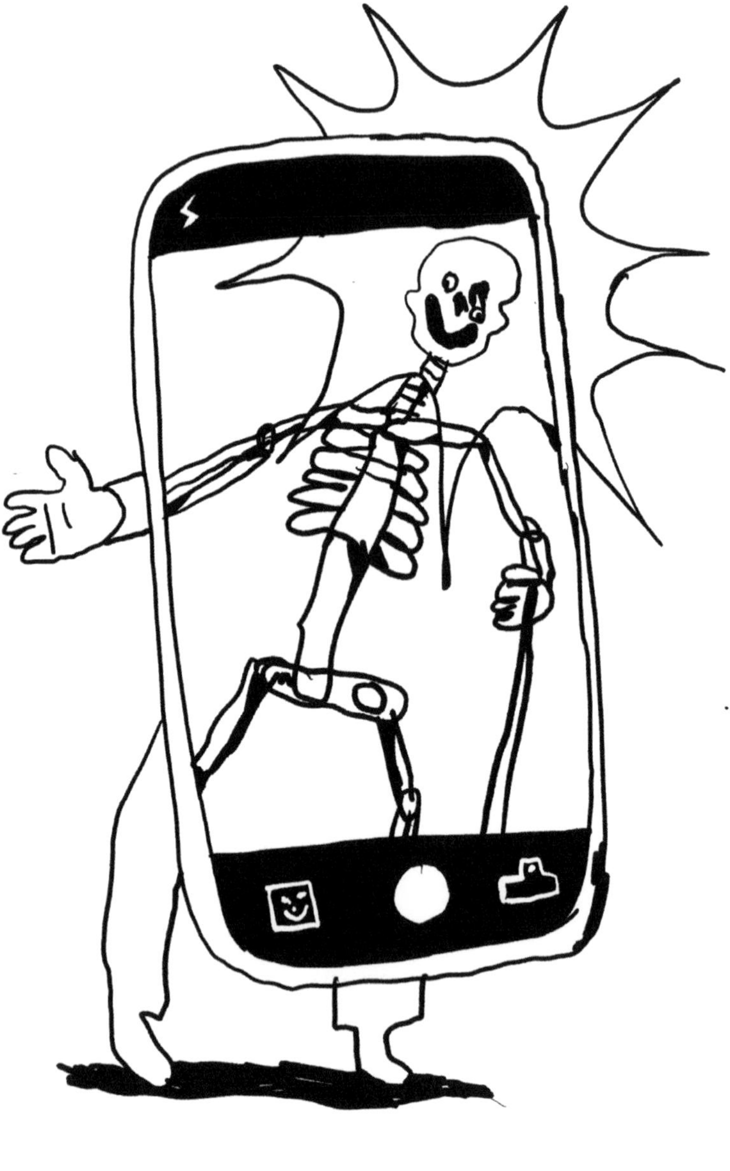

SELFIE ABUSE

Apparently my life is not worth much -
It's not been happy snapped. Observers sense
I must have failed to come to something, such
Is my avoidance of the evidence
I should present to prove that I had fun.
But frankly, I forgot the photo op.
No, not forgot, forswore. I chose to shun
It all, and live without that mindless prop -
The pleasure stick - that fingers grasp until
An image splashes out, a frantic mess
Of mini me. I know they love the thrill
Of shop / hill / actor / concert / lioness -
Photographer in front and star behind -
And yet they miss so much. They're going blind.

MY PRIVATE VIEW

I've often seen a painting as a trap
To fall in for the blissless unaware.
A 'landscape' eh? I need a contoured map
To follow as I wonder everywhere.
Club members do not drink, no, they "imbibe"
While passing round the plate of petit fame;
And once admitted, they are free to jibe
At panic-stricken outcasts. "Such a shame,
Can you not feel the line of carefree hand?
The ageing sun? The solid sea?" (It's pink!)
I cannot listen to this servile band -
They talk in tongues. What do they think we think?
Well I think I should take that carefree line
And shove it where the ageing sun don't shine.

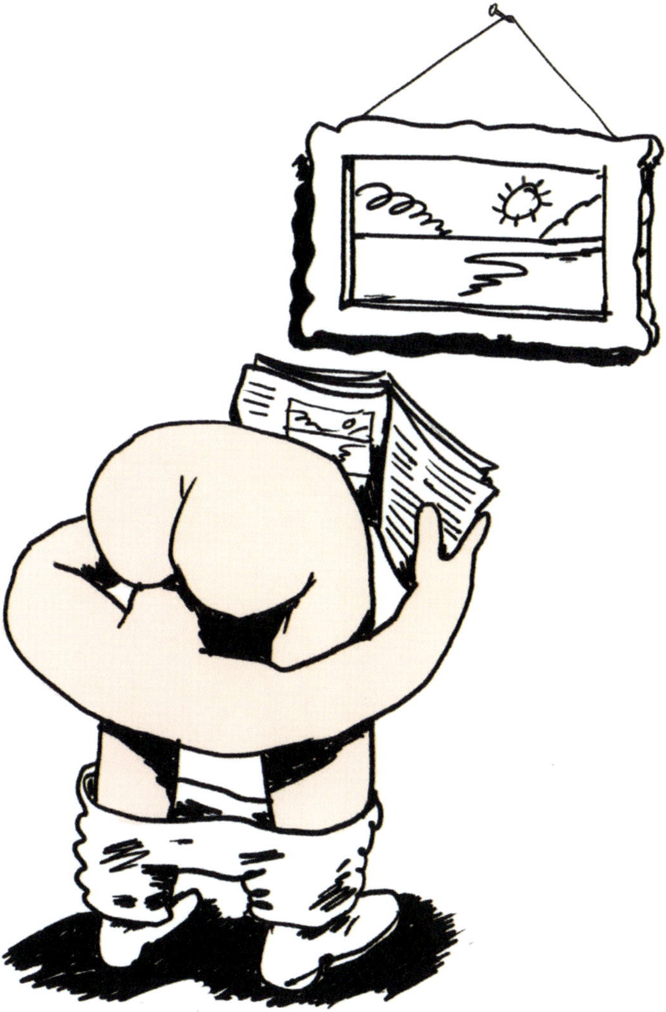

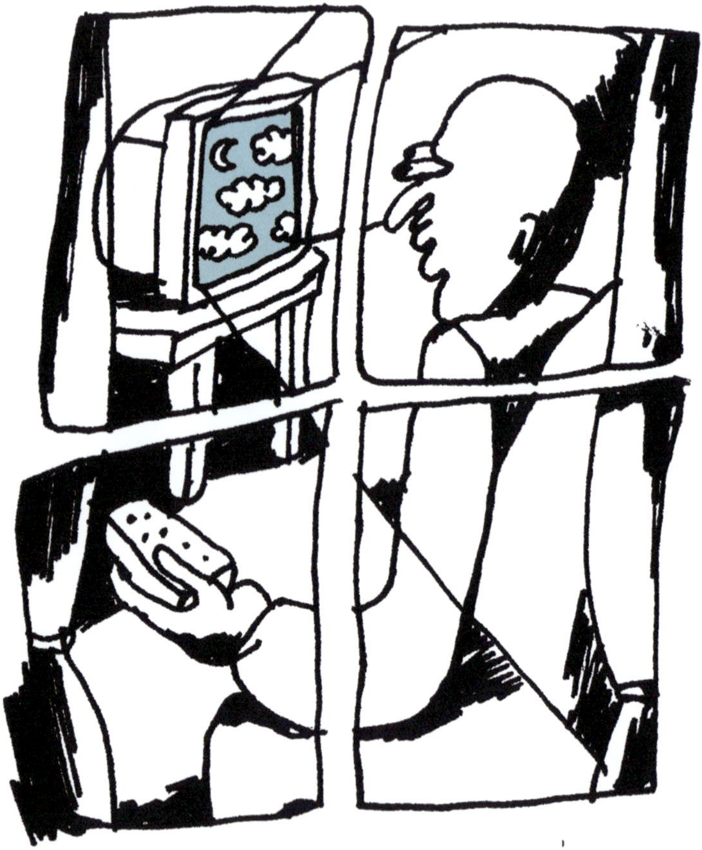

SCREENED OFF

The amber of the evening melts away
And wearily the sun sets down its light.
Begrudgingly it hides its fire away
And bows its head. It's fact that makes you bright.
From where you sit you watch red, green and blue -
The dots which dash their message: 'Be aware!
We're bringing you a panoramic view.'
(A panorama in a tiny square?)
The colours that you see are fast, now seen
As words that have been written in a book;
Transmitted, set in stone upon the screen,
While rainbows fade away. Why should you look
At silver moonbeams dancing on the floor?
Just draw the curtains. You'll see so much more.

QUESTIONABLE TIME

Yes, well said Mr Panellist, I'm sure
Your observation's fair. But it's not right
That those wool-headed punters on the floor
Applaud you 'til eternity. Tonight
I'd like some straight opinions please, not stats
That any politician can respin
To match a manifesto. No more spats
Or toys and prams please - you will never win
Me over that way. As you hurl your voice,
Inciting ovine bleating in the hall,
My isolated chair gives me the choice
To sit in peace. I'll never cheer at all
At your behest; instead I'll take a nap
And dream perchance you get another clap.

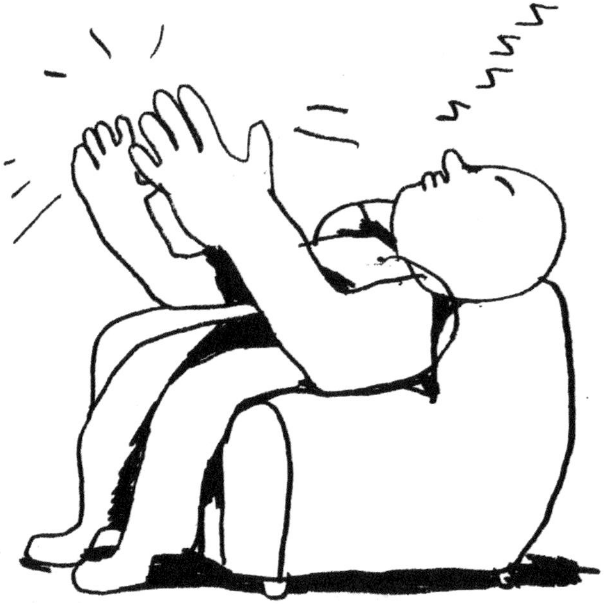

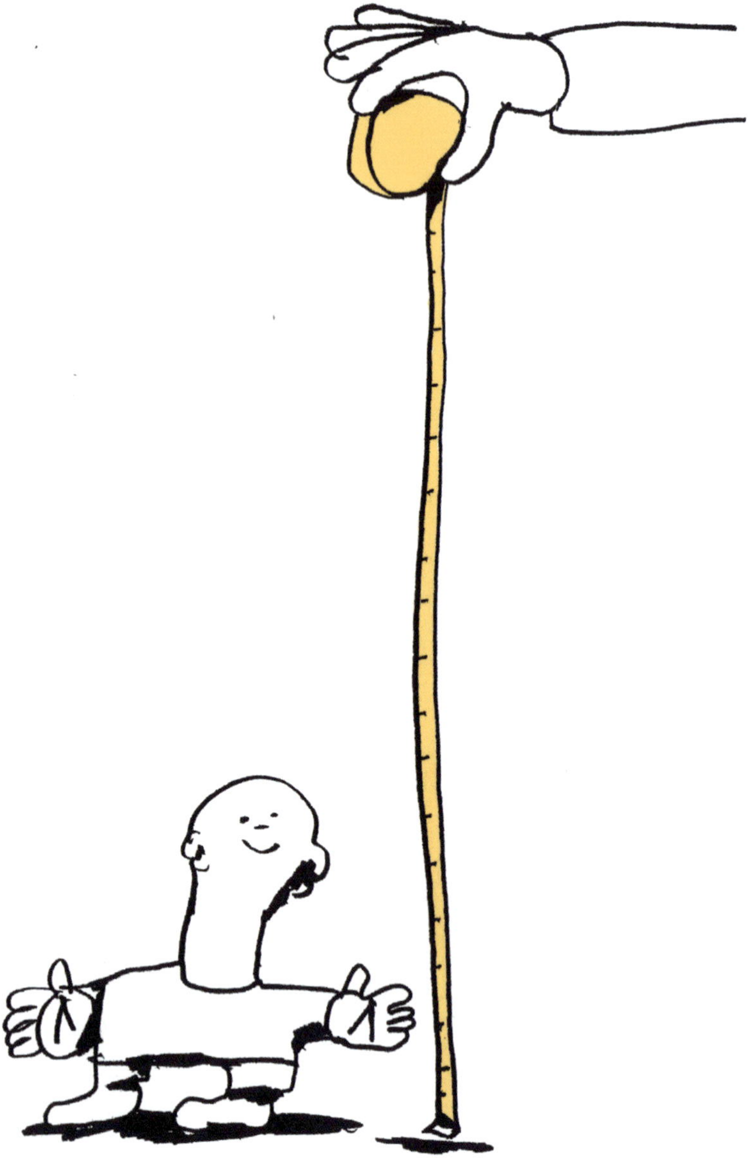

BRAVO OSCAR

We had a vote one Sunday lunch to choose
The tallest in the family. It might
Seem odd, but once we'd counted up the views
Of how we saw our kin, it wasn't height
That counted highest. No, that would be wrong.
Longevity is critical, and so
Is who you did and didn't get along
With when the tiffs broke out. It's good to know
It's fair. At the Academy they built
The prototype, where leading stars believe
Their prize sets them apart. They feel no guilt
Their film took less, as this would be naive.
They say it's just a laugh, and they are right,
But they forget they're [sic] jokes on the night.

BAD
SPORT

EFF ONE

The wheels and cars go round and round. And round.
And all the world tunes in to see which one
Will take the chequered flag today. I'm bound
To say I won't be joining in the fun.
I know all F1 followers will claim
Excitement doesn't come more charged than this,
But any race I see feels just the same
As any race before. Is it remiss
Of me to knock it for its senselessness?
I can't tell who the leader is. The air
Exudes environmental recklessness.
The noise is so much more than I can bear.
And as a thousand pit lane experts fix
The cars, they give the race its name. Grand Prix.

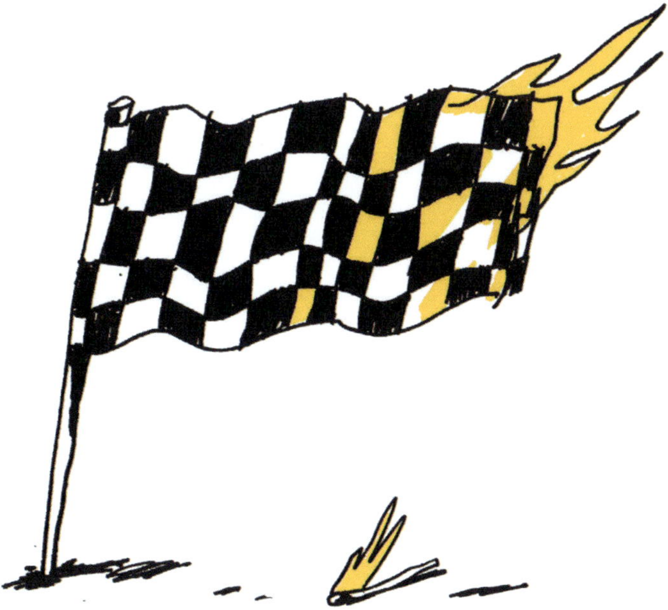

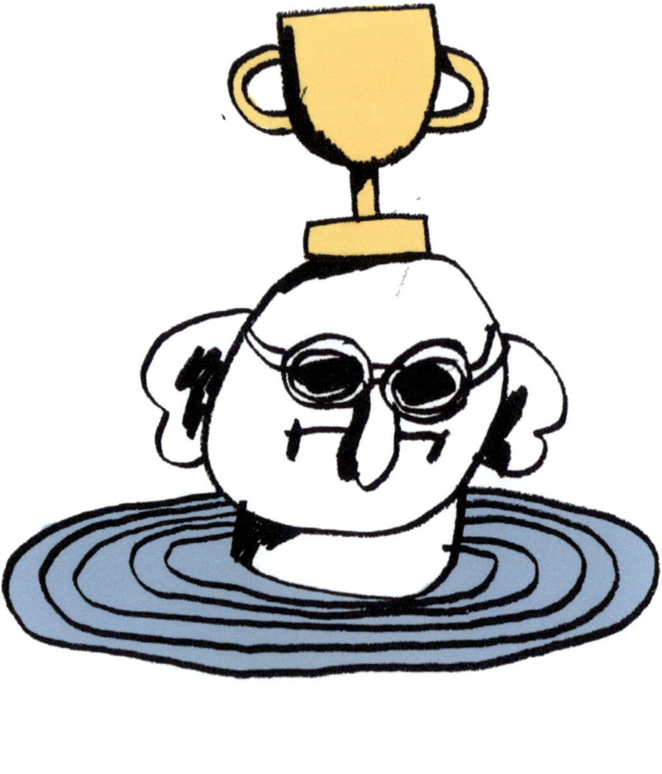

TALENT POOL

"Your PB for the hundred is?" I said,
As Freshman Athlete waited for the gun.
"It all depends on where I put my head,"
He answered. *"Pointing skyward as I run?*
Or chin against my chest, reducing drag?"
"Just choose the one you're best at, on the flat."
"I do both." "Yes, but surely you're a stag
One way, and slug the other." *"You know that*
I can run backwards too?" "But that won't win
If other athletes run the front-on way."
"I also hop like Peter Rabbit. Spin
Like Nureyev. All win a prize, they say."
"I'm sorry, this is not a swimming pool;
On track there's just one medal, just one rule."

ALTIUS – ISH

When man created all the ancient sports
In Grecian times, three thousand years ago,
He had a single purpose for his thoughts:
Establishing advantage over foe.
So skills were mainly martial, while the rules
(And clothing too) were minimal. We still
Play ancient games today, but fossil fools
Have meddled with the finer points until
They've screwed them up completely. Now we're bound
By high jump rules which say you have to make
Your leap from one foot only on the ground.
And you can land back-first. It's sure to break!
A gymnast, off two feet, achieves more height
And lands quite safely, ready for the fight.

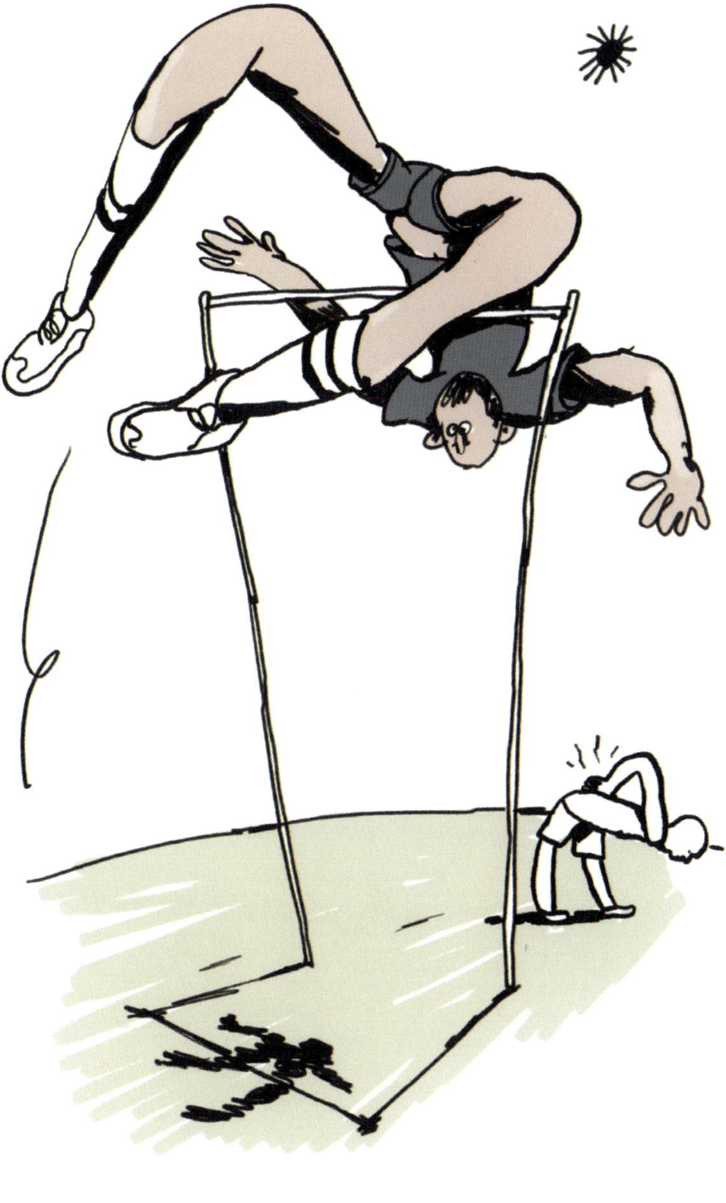

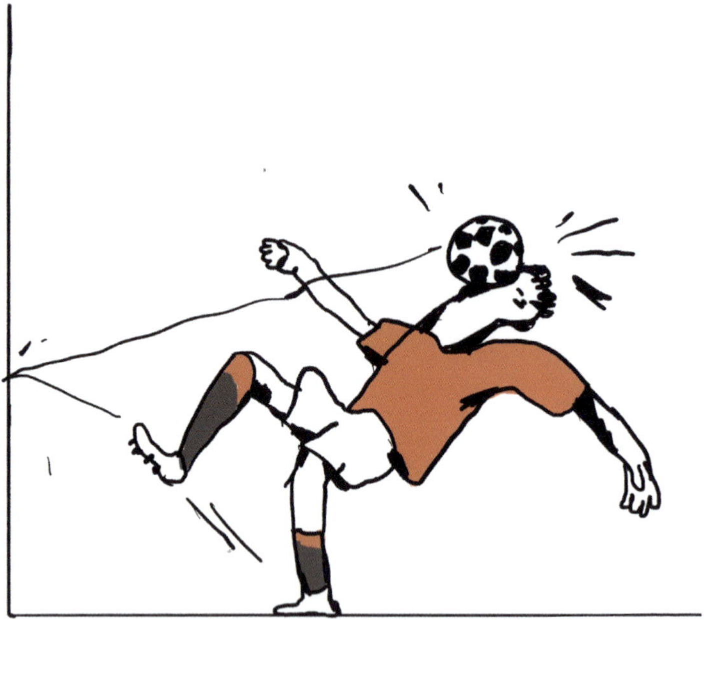

MAN U

Those Manchester United fans, eh? They
Are not born near the Theatre of Dreams
Where ghosts of Edwards, Byrne and Best still play.
They could have chosen weaker, local teams
But they're convinced to play the Man U game
By marketing machines on the attack.
For youngsters I suppose it is a shame,
As once they fall in love there's no way back.
And even if they find the team next door
Comes calling, they will cast its love aside;
When you are used to silver, knowing you're
Avoiding relegation brings no pride.
And how the ManUfactory till schtings
As parents buy up countless useless things.

GREEN EYES

I've moaned about the ancient fools before
In other sports, but special mention goes
To those with Royal title. Wanting more
From life - quite why, though, only heaven knows -
Than leather chairs and single malts, they've moved
To outlaw certain ways of holing out.
I don't suppose our lives will be improved.
We all know golf is tough enough without
Such silliness. For every other shot
You do your very best to hit the ball
Whichever way you choose. But this does not
Hold true for putting - refs must be on call.
No anchor points. No through-the-legs address.
It makes no odds, it's just a spiteful mess.

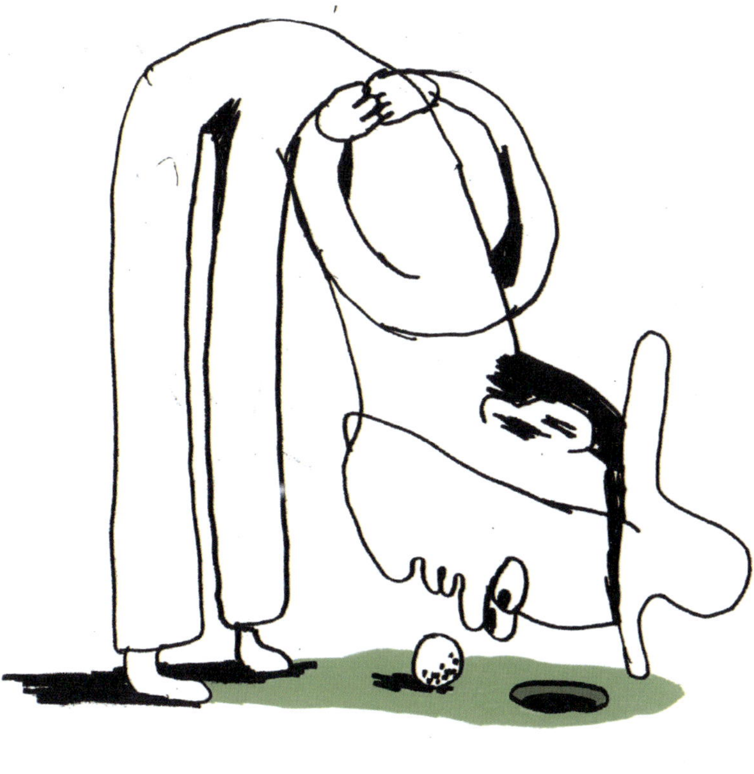

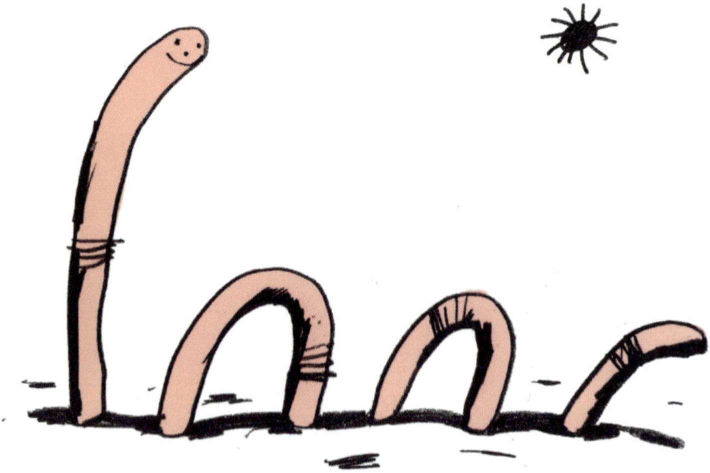

THE WORM-CAST

Out walking on the shore one summer's day
I nearly saw a never-ebbing tide
On land which nature sculpted for our play.
I'd climbed the dunes and on the other side
A mortal winner, thirty-two short years
Ago, was here again to say goodbye.
He understood and waved farewell to cheers,
But found himself the CGOTY-
In-waiting once again. Immortal soon.
Could one man-moment harness the goodwill
To win on this romantic afternoon?
Or could a bleeding piece of earth now kill
The dream? That bloody worm-cast won the day.
The bounce was bad. The tide tiptoed away.

WHAT'S THE POINT?

Has football's level playing field been tipped?
A three-point win but one point for a draw?
It's out of true, and just last year it ripped
The fairness from the season's final score.
The game is pure, so what does logic lack
That it is overlooked? Two teams, one ball,
Two goals. But turn defence into attack
And maths turns into magic as it all
Goes pear-shaped. Surely ruling bodies should
Give points for what the game is all about.
A one-point draw is plainly half as good
As any win - a close one or a rout.
But City took top spot from Liverpool
As one plus one makes three is now the rule.

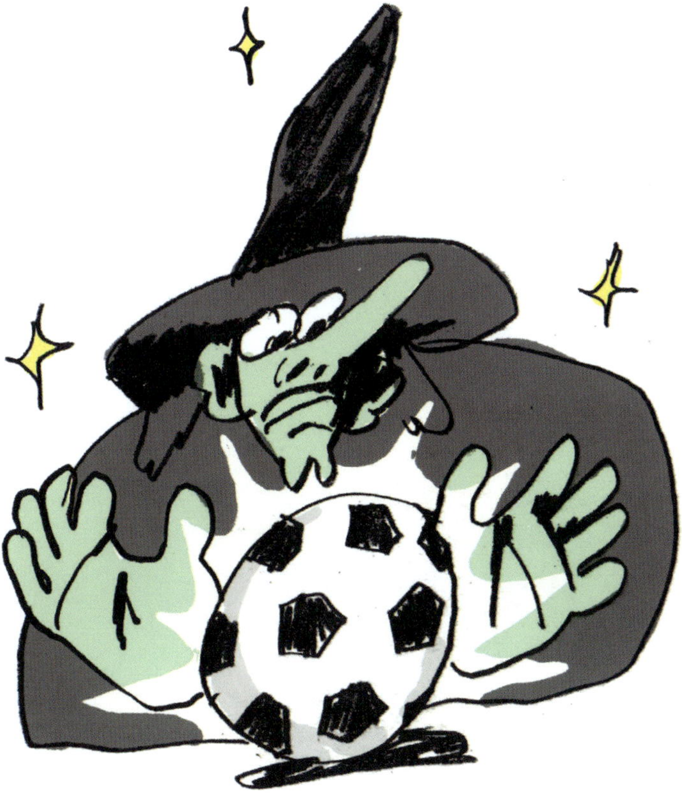

LAST WORDS

TIME WASTING

A cancelled meeting takes my living hours
Away from me. I thought I was supposed
To travel - I had read it in my stars -
What stupid dead words, lying in their rows.
A futile trek with nothing at the end
Is covered in a distant, vacant gaze;
A silent, empty gap sits where a friend

Might well have helped to occupy the days.
So now I want to win that lost time back.
Perhaps I could pretend that, while away,
I'm gaining no experience, and lack
The proof of some achievement here today.
But in the end I thought I'd write a rhyme
And now you know I've wasted all your time.

Greg Tustain

Since achieving a C in his English 'O' level, Greg has been trying to improve his writing, mainly as a copywriter for various London advertising agencies.

This collection of soddets is the result of a lifetime spent trying to understand lots of things not very well, getting cross with them for the tiniest of reasons, and then being unable to go into too much detail when asked to explain why.

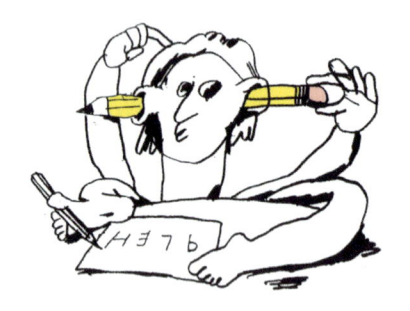

Harry Wyld

Harry is an artist and scribbler happy working across multiple mediums and subject matters - even the gripes of a grumpy old codger.

He was on the beach in New Zealand when Greg's email pinged into his inbox. On the other side of the world, toes in the sand and Soddet in hand, home had never felt so close.